# JAVASCRIPT

*Beginner JavaScript Coding from*
*The Ground Up*

# Table of Contents

# CHAPTER 1

# INTRODUCTION TO JAVASCRIPT

JavaScript is known as the "language of the web" because it is used in the development of an incredibly high number of applications on the web and the mobile paradigm alike. It is the language which makes web applications dynamic so that users can interact with them, which provides a rich user experience.

When JavaScript came into existence around 1995, most of the logical calculations and input validations in web pages were primarily done using server-side languages like PHP. The process was very long and unnecessarily involved two-way trips, first to send a request to the server and then get the data/error back to the client's computer. It was a huge letdown to UX. The need of that time was to make validations right on the client's computer before sending to the server, thereby reducing the bandwidth, which at that time was a major issue so that the user would not have to wait just to see if he made any errors while typing out that form.

JavaScript was created by Brendan Eich as "LiveScript" in 1995, which got renamed to "JavaScript." It was initially named "Mocha" but then named JavaScript to gain traction with the language Java that was getting popular at the same time. The first major standardization occurred in the form of ECMA standardization. The first version developed still lacked features like REGEX and JSON and some important built-in functions. The language kept getting developed and adding features to its repertoire.

It was the ECMA v3 that saw the birth of AJAX (Asynchronous JavaScript and XML), which today is at the core of every web application and framework.

At present, the language is packed with exciting new features. Let's look at the advantages one gets with JavaScript:

- JavaScript is a lightweight, interpreted programming language.
- Designed for creating simple as well as complex web applications

- Furthers the functionality of web pages
- Animations and Visual effects can be done easily
- UI/UX improvements

Owing to the language's success and usability, many frameworks and libraries like jQuery, Angular JS, React JS have been developed which make writing code in JavaScript a delight.

JavaScript is the scripting language that is being actively used by developers around the globe in creating interactive web applications that are visually appealing and at the same time packed with functionalities just like the desktop applications are.

It means that web pages are not static in nature. The elements can be modified and made interactive, functional and animated by the use of this language as a scripting tool.

JavaScript began as a client-side scripting language but is being used on the backend side of the web also in the form of Node.js. Many libraries and frameworks have sprung up in the meantime to make the developer's life easy.

JavaScript has built-in as well as user-defined methods/functions that allow themselves to get bound to certain buttons or elements and can be called whenever and wherever. These functions are being actively used to automate tasks like the setTimeout() or setInterval() functions that can be called after a certain period of time to do some task.JavaScript can be used in the HTML file itself, if it is written into the <script> tags, and can also be attached to it as an external file. The extension of a JavaScript program is '.js.'

JavaScript is often abbreviated as JS. Some of the main features of the language are as follows:

- High-level, Weakly Typed
- Interpreted
- Functional
- Object-Oriented

Object-Oriented design is perhaps the most important feature of JavaScript, as it allows us the creation of objects and establishes relationships between them, commonly known as Inheritance and Encapsulation, which you'll come to know about in the proceeding chapters.

CHAPTER 2

# MAIN FEATURES OF JAVASCRIPT

Most of the features of JavaScript are more or less same as that of other common programming languages. Almost all the programming languages have these features. The main features are as follows.

1. **JavaScript Variables**

   One of the very important features of JavaScript is variables. They act as the storage containers for values. In other words, they are the names of the memory locations at which the values are stored. These values can be an integer, decimal values, strings or single characters. The variable names have to be unique. This is important because otherwise, this will create a great amount of confusion. The name of the variable can start from an alphabet, dollar sign or underscore signs.

The names are case-sensitive. You will get to know exact rules for naming a variable in the later chapter.

Examples of some variables are:

var abcd;
var $abc;

2. **JavaScript Objects**

Objects are nothing but a collection of some data values. These generally are written as name-value pairs. For example:

var name = {firstName:"Amit",
            lastName:"Kumar",
            age:70};

To access the values in an object, we use dot notation. For example, if you want to access the lastName present in name object, we can write that as name.lastName. Arrays are a type of object.

3. **JavaScript Comments**

Comment is a feature which is often neglected by novice programmers, but as one starts getting experienced at coding, they realize the great value it brings to the code. These are basically a way to create notes in the code. This improves the readability of the code. They are not executed by the compiler.

There are two types of comments:
a.  Single line comments
b.  Multi-line comments
   a.  Single line comments
       This as the name suggests, is used when the comments are single line
       For example:
       var name;      //name of the customer
   b.  Multi-line comments
       This is used if the length of the comment goes beyond a line. For example:
       /* This program calculates
       the factorial of a number
       */

## 4.  JavaScript Functions or methods

Functions form an integral part of any programming language. Function helps us write code in an efficient manner which not only improves the readability but also contribute a great deal while maintaining it. A function is a set of statements which are used to carry out a particular task. For example:

```
function addTwoNumbers(num1, num2) {

        return num1+num2; //Calculates     and
        returns the sum
}
```

You will learn about functions in detail in later chapters.

5. **Conditional statements**

Conditional statements are used when we need to make certain decisions based on some conditions. For example, if there is a program to find out if a person is eligible to vote or not, we input the age of the person and compare it with 18. If it is more than 18, we say that person is eligible to vote or else not.

For example:

```
if(age>18)
        alert ("eligible to vote");
else
        alert ("Ineligible to vote");
```

## 6. Looping constructs in JavaScript

Loops are used to execute a certain part of code several times repeatedly. There are various ways in which we can implement loops. E.g. For loop, while loop, do-while loop.

For example:

```
for (i = 0; i < 10; i++)
{
   alert(i);
}
```

## 7. Event handling in JavaScript

Events are some activity which happens on the web page. For example, a mouse click on the web page, loading of the web page, etc. Event handling is a way to handle what happens when such event occurs. Some common event handlers are onclick, onload, onmouseover, and onmouseout. This is a very important concept. Developing any web application without event handlers does not make any sense.

This chapter talks about the main features of JavaScript in short. The later chapters of this book explain these features in great detail.

# CHAPTER 3

# REAL-LIFE USES OF JAVASCRIPT

JavaScript is being used on almost every website out there on the web, and why not? It adds so much functionality to any page that uses this scripting language. If it wasn't for JavaScript, we would probably be stuck in the 90s where websites offered no functionalities to the users. It was not at all intuitive as far as user-experience (UX) is concerned, which is perhaps the best thing that this language has given to us.

JavaScript is practically everywhere. From the forms that you submit to the drop-down buttons on the menus of the modern websites to the numerous errors that it shows when you leave a field blank to the most annoying yet useful alert boxes, they all are made using JavaScript.

By now, you probably would have guessed what JavaScript brings to the table.

Yes, everything.

Learning the basic, simple syntax of the language can give you the power to build a whole calculator that looks decent enough, and in case you happen to sprinkle a little of the CSS magic, that would look just amazing. And that is where the practical usage of the language literally begins.

Let's look at some practical, real-life scenarios where JavaScript has proved to be a boon:

# Case 1: Form Validation

A good form on the internet is said to be that one that utilizes the power of JavaScript to validate user-input and display errors whenever there is an empty field, or inappropriate field inputs occur. Let's assume the case if JavaScript was not used here. In that case, the user who is filling the form would have to first submit the form, and since he does not know whether he's made any errors yet, and when it is submitted, it is sent to the server to be processed by a POST request, and then the server responds with any error(s) that might have occurred. This is a two-way trip.

Much of this can be saved if we use client-side validation using JavaScript. And here comes the power of JavaScript when it responds in split seconds if the user makes any error(s) while filling the form itself.

## Case 2: DOM Manipulation

Most of the time, the server responds with a static web page that the browser renders and displays it on the browser. But, what if we get the power to manipulate a few elements on the web page? Wouldn't it feel exciting if we could change the state of things, their order, their properties and even their attributes and it could become a whole new thing altogether? Well, it turns out JavaScript does give us all that might to make all that happen. Pretty sweet.

## Case 3: Event Listeners

The only way a user truly gets engaged with a web page is when they are allowed to click a button and they get a response back, like some new page or it changes some data on the web page, or it allows them to carry out some calculation on-the-fly. JavaScript allows us to add that functionality by attaching functions to buttons or elements on the web page, often called DOM (Document

Object Model) elements that bind themselves to that element and only execute or fire when the requisite action is carried out. This makes the user-experience satisfied.

There are many uses of JavaScript that are adding to the rich UX of the web pages. In the modern websites, nowadays, Client Side Rendering has made way for a new category of web pages called as Single Page Applications (SPAs) that are capable of generating HTML pages on the fly by using JSON data from the server only. This has bridged the gap between the frontend and the backend of web development.

The future of the web looks bright in the hands of JavaScript.

CHAPTER 4

# YOUR FIRST JAVASCRIPT PROGRAM

HTML adds structure to a web page and CSS (Cascading Style Sheets) adds the relevant style required to make the page look elegant.

But, how do you make the page talk? How do you make it dynamic?

That's where JavaScript comes in.

JavaScript adds additional functionality to a rather static web page and lets users interact with the various elements present in the page.

In this chapter, you'll make your very first JavaScript program, the famous "Hello, World!" that will introduce you to this vast yet simple language that is often touted as the "Language of the Web." It is presumed here that you are aware of HTML and CSS syntax, as they'll be used throughout the text.

Web Browsers render HTML and CSS and display it on the screen, and have a built-in JavaScript interpreter that understands the language and executes the tasks of the program.

But for browsers to know where to start with the interpretation of JavaScript, we need to make use of the <script> tag that tells the browser the starting point of the program. </script> tells the browser that it has reached the end of the program.

JavaScript is written within the tags <script> and </script>, and these tags are most commonly placed just above the </body> tag.

This is done to make the script load after the initial page-load that makes the page load faster.

## Your first program

Let's create a program that makes an alert box with the message "Hello, World!".

```
<html>
<head>
      <title> First Program </title>
</head>
<body>
      <h1>This is your first JavaScript program </h1>
      <script>
      // This is a comment
      alert('Hello World!');
      </script>
</body>
</html>
```

**Screenshot of the result:**

If you're using a modern browser like Chrome or Firefox or Safari, they support HTML5. But if you're on an old browser which does not support HTML5, you'll need to add the attribute of *type* to the <script> tag, and it'll look like this:

<script type="text/javascript">...</script>

// ->This tells the browser that a comment will follow and ignore the line. This is particularly useful to document your code so that anyone is able to understand what you've written.

JavaScript has various inbuilt functions, which you can think of as little pre-written programs designed to do some tasks. One such function that we have used in our first JavaScript program is the alert() function.

The alert() function takes in a string in between the parentheses and displays an alert box showing that text.

Here, we want the alert box to say "Hello, World!". So, we have written "Hello, World!" inside the parentheses.

Congratulations! You have just made your very first JavaScript program. While JavaScript offers many functionalities, this was one to let you get started with the language that is aptly said to be the language of the web.

# CHAPTER 5

# EMBEDDING JAVASCRIPT CODE IN HTML

You can use JavaScript with HTML for a dynamic and delightful user experience. In this chapter, we will learn about the various ways through which we can embed JavaScript in an HTML document.

In order to embed JavaScript directly in a page, you can use the <script> tag.

The syntax of the script tag is as follows:

```
<script>

//JavaScript code goes here, example:

alert("Hello from JavaScript");

</script>
```

Various optional attributes are available for use with the script tag for more customization. Here is the list of available attributes that can be used with the tag:

**type:** This tag is used to specify the language written between the script tag, but since JavaScript is the primary scripting language used for all web browsers, it is not mandatory to use this attribute, as it is set by default. Here is an example:

```
<script type="text/JavaScript">

//JavaScript code here

</script>
```

**src:** If you want to load JavaScript code externally then this is the attribute which you should be looking at. The URL of the external JavaScript code is set as the value of this attribute.

```
<script src="url/to/external/JavaScript/file.js"></script>
```

**defer:** If this attribute is present in the script tag then the JavaScript file associated with script tag is executed after the page has been fully parsed, i.e. after the DOMContentLoaded event is fired. Example:

```
<script src="path/to/file.js" defer></script>
```

Note that this attribute is only for JavaScript code loaded externally, i.e., if the src attribute is present in the same script tag as the defer attribute.

**async:** If this attribute is present in the script tag then the JavaScript file associated with script tag is executed asynchronously while the page continues to load. If this tag is not present then the script is first executed, and then the page load continues. Example:

```
<script src="path/to/file.js" async></script>
```

Note that this attribute is only for JavaScript code loaded externally, i.e., if the src attribute is present in the same script tag as the defer attribute.

There is one more way to embed JavaScript in HTML, which is to write JavaScript code in event handler attributes of elements. This way when that event fires, the JavaScript code which has been written as the attribute value is executed!

```
<button onclick="alert('JavaScript from event handler');">Click me</button>
```

In the above example when the button is clicked an alert dialog pops up with the message "JavaScript from event handler," showing that the JavaScript in attribute value was executed.

Do not worry if you could not understand the above code example. Events and event handler attributes are discussed in detail later in this book.

So that was all for this chapter, now you are ready to embed JavaScript into your HTML document and make it more awesome!

# BASIC DISPLAY OPERATIONS IN JAVASCRIPT

Following are some of the ways by which JavaScript displays data:

- Writing into an HTML element, using **innerHTML**.
- Writing into the HTML output using **document.write ()**.
- Writing into an alert box, using **window.alert ()**.
- Writing into the browser console, using **console.log ()**.

# innerHTML

"innerHTML" as the name suggests, represents the inner content of an HTML element. So basically we can use innerHTML property to change the content inside any HTML element. However, there is a small catch. How will the JavaScript know which element we are actually interested in changing? What if it changes the content of all the elements present in the web page? To solve this problem, we assign an id to the HTML element whose content we are interested in changing. That way we will be sure as to which element should reflect the changes. The next situation which arises in front of us is how we access an HTML element based on the id. In such case, we make use of a method called document.getElementById ("ID").

Changing the innerHTML property of an HTML element is a common way to display data in HTML.

Let us look at an example here.

```
<!DOCTYPE html>
<html>
<body>

<h1>Chapter 6</h1>
<p>Use of innerHTML to display data</p>

<p id="new"></p>
```

```
<script>
document.getElementById ("new").innerHTML = "This
is how it's done";

</script>
</body>
</html>
```

## document.write ()

Another interesting way to display data in a web page
using JavaScript is document.write (). The complete web
page can be termed as a document. So as the name of this
function suggests, it is used to write on the document. If
it is used after the page is loaded, it not only writes but
also replaces the existing (old) value with the new one.
Therefore, one should be very careful while working
with them. It is mainly used for testing purposes.

Let's understand this through an example:

```
<!DOCTYPE html>
<html>
<body>
```

```
<h1>Chapter 6</h1>
<p>Use of document.write() to display data</p>

<script>
document.write(1+2);
</script>

</body>
</html>
```

As I was saying, using document.write () after an HTML document is fully loaded will **delete all existing HTML.** Let us see this through an example

```
<!DOCTYPE html>
<html>
<body>

<h1>My First Web Page</h1>
<p>My first paragraph.</p>
<button onclick="document.write (1+2)"> Magic Button!!
</button>

</body>
```

</html>

# window.alert ()

You have probably seen on many websites an alert like "You seem to have entered a wrong password." These appear in the form of small dialog boxes and are often used to alert the user of something.

```
<!DOCTYPE html>
<html>
<body>

<h1>My First Web Page</h1>
<p>My first paragraph.</p>

<button onclick="window.alert(1+2)">Add 1 & 2</button>

</body>
</html>
```

# console.log ()

"console.log ()" is a savior for developers. It is used for debugging purposes. The result from console.log () is not displayed on the web page. Instead, it is displayed in the console. This is a useful feature because sometimes you don't want testing data to be displayed on the web page. Those data are used by the developer to know if everything is working fine on the website or not. In case you are wondering what a console looks like, press ctrl+shift+I in Google Chrome on the desired web page.

```
<!DOCTYPE html>
<html>
<body>

<script>
console.log("it is in console");
</script>

</body>
</html>
```

You will get more familiar with console.log () when you start creating applications in JavaScript.

The above were the four ways in which we display data in JavaScript. However, it must be kept in mind that their usage depends on the requirement. You need to select the required method based on the desired result.

# CHAPTER 7

# VARIABLES, DATA TYPES & CONSTANTS

# Variables

Variables are always an important aspect of any programming language. They are used to store values which can be later addressed using those variable names. Same goes with JavaScript. Let us look at the syntax for creating a variable:

**Syntax**

var <variableName>;        //Declares a variable
<variableName> = value;    //Assigning value to the variable

Or

var <variableName> = value; //Declaration and assignment in same line

In the first method, we declare the variable first and then assign a value to it at some later point in the program. The only thing one must keep in mind here is that declaration must always come before the assignment. However, in the second method, both the declaration as well as the assignment happen in a single line.

Let us look at some examples here

var abc;                    //Declaration
abc = "New variable";       // Assignment
var num = 33;               //Declaration and
                            assignment

In above example, the variable "abc" will store the string value "New variable" while the variable "num" will store the number value 33.

Let us look at one more example:

var marksScience = 85; //Variable name
var marksMaths= 100;
var total = marksScience+ marksMaths; //add and store the result
In the above example,the variable total will store the calculated value i.e. 185.

All the variables which are used in the program must have unique names or else it might end up creating a ruckus while executing the code. These unique names are called identifiers. For naming a variable, certain rules must be followed.

**Rules for naming a variable**

- Names must start with a letter, dollar ($), or underscore (_).
- You can include letters, digits, underscores, and dollar signs in a variable name.
- Variable names in JavaScript are case-sensitive.
- You cannot use reserved words / keywords as variable names.

Some of the examples of valid variable names are as follows:

Marks1
$abc
_fun
marks2

You would have noticed that we make use of an "equal to" symbol to assign some values to a variable. This "equal to" symbol is called assignment operator and is used to initialize a variable.

**Few important points to remember:**

1.  When you simply declare a variable, it holds no value.
    For example:

    var abc;

    Here the variable "abc" will not contain any value until we assign it some value.

2.  Many variables can be declared in a single statement. To do that, we start the statement with var and separate the variables by a comma.
    For example:

    var firstName="Amitabh", lastName ="Kumar", age=70;

3.  The declaration of variables can span multiple lines.

    var firstName="Amitabh",

lastName ="Kumar",
age=70;

4. Most of the time, variables are simply declared and are initialized at some later point in the program. As mentioned in the first point, after the declaration, the variable holds no value. To be precise, it holds the value **undefined**. For example:

var name;

The variable "name" will contain the value undefined after the above statement is executed.

5. Even if you re-declare a JavaScript variable, it retains its previous value.

For example:

var name="Amitabh";
var name;

Even after the execution of these statements, the variable "name" will still have the value "Amitabh."

# Data Types

Data types, as the name suggests, signifies the type of data a variable can hold. A JavaScript variable can hold several types of data. For example string, number, object, Boolean, etc.

```
var age = 70                    //stores a Number
var lastName = "Kumar"          // stores a String
var name = {firstName:"Amitabh", lastName:"Kumar"};
                                // stores an object
var case=true; //Stores a Boolean
```

Data types is an important aspect of programming because it specifies what kind of data a variable is holding. This helps the compiler to understand what kind of operations can be performed on them. The addition operator will have different results if applied to two numbers and a radically different result if applied on two strings. For example:

```
var name ="Amit" + ""+ "Kumar";
```

```
var age = 30+40;
```

The variable "name" will store the concatenated value of both the strings i.e. "Amit Kumar" while the variable age will store the added value of 30 & 40 i.e. 70.

Now consider the next example:

var abc = 70 + "Amit";

If we try and relate the above example with normal arithmetic, it does not makes much sense. Adding a number to a string is not possible in normal arithmetic. However, it would be interesting to see how JavaScript will treat the above example. JavaScript will interpret the above example as follows:

var abc = "70" + "Amit";

Whenever we try to add a number with a string, JavaScript will treat the number as a string. However, what if our expression is a mix of several numbers and several strings! What will be the result in that case? Let's look at the following two examples:

var temp = "Amit" + " " + "Kumar" + 30 + 40;
var temp1 = 30 + 40 +"Amit" + " " + "Kumar" ;


In the above examples, the temp will store the value "Amit Kumar3040" whereas the variable temp1 will store "70Amit Kumar". How similar looking expressions produced different results? Let's see how JavaScript treats the above two example. JavaScript starts evaluating expressions from left to right. So in the first case when it encountered a string, it considers all the remaining as a string itself. Therefore 30 and 40 becomes two separate strings. However, in the second example, since the numbers are written first, it first adds them and then concatenates with the remaining string.

Before we dive into each type of JavaScript data types, I must point out that JavaScript has dynamic types. Let me explain it to you what that means. In C language, we use data types such as int, float, char, etc. Those are static data types which mean they cannot take any other type of value during the execution of the program. However, we see no such types here. We simply declare a variable using the keyword "var" and then go on to mutate it the way want. Even if we have stored a string value in the variable, at some later point in the program, we can assign a number to it. Therefore the types in JavaScript are dynamic in nature. For example:

```
var rand;                //rand is undefined
var rand= "Random";      //rand stores an string
var rand= 70;            //Now rand stores a number
```

Now that we have looked at properties of data types let's look at each data types in detail.

There are two kinds of data types in JavaScript:

a.   Primitive data

b.   Non-primitive or complex data

Primitive is the predefined types of data which are inbuilt to a language. There are five primitive data types in JavaScript:

- String
- Number
- Boolean
- Null
- Undefined

Non-primitive or complex data are not provided by default but are defined by the programmer. For example arrays, objects, etc.

## Strings

Strings are nothing but a series of characters. They are either enclosed in single or double quotes. Addition operation on them is nothing but a simple concatenation.

For example:

var name = "Ämit Kumar";
var name2= 'Javed';

Quotes inside a string are not a problem as long as they are different than the quotes surrounding the string. For example:

var xyz = "It's done";

var xyz1 = 'Friends call him "James"';

# Numbers

Unlike most of the other programming language, JavaScript does not have a concept of integer, float, etc. Instead, it just has a single concept of numbers which may or may not contain decimals

var   x   =   74.00;                    //    Decimals
var y = 33;      // Without decimals

If the number is extremely large, it can be written using scientific notation. For example:

var   x   =   333e5;                    //    33300000
var y = 23e-5;    // 0.00023

# Booleans

The concept of Boolean is almost same as that of other programming languages. Booleans have only two values

– "true" and "false." The major use of these comes while forming conditional statements.

```
var a = true;
var b = false;
```

# Null

Null means "nothing." The value null signifies the intentional absence of any object value. An object can be emptied by setting it to null.

```
var name=null;        //value becomes null
```

# Undefined

The variables which are not assigned any value will contain undefined. For example:

```
var abc; // value is undefined
```

We can also assign the value "undefined" to a variable.

```
abc= undefined;
```

People generally get confused between null and undefined. I will explain the difference at some later point in this chapter.

Those were the primitive types. Now let us look at some non-primitive data types.

# Arrays

Arrays are nothing but a collection of some values. The set of those values is written using curly braces. Like all other programming language, the index starts with 0.

```
var names[ ] = { "Ram", "Rahim", "Jaspaal"};

//names[0]="Ram";
```

# Objects

Objects in JavaScript are written as name- value pairs. For example:

```
var name = {firstName:"Amit",
                lastName:"Kumar",
                age:70};
```

Before I close in on the discussion on data types, I must explain about an operator called "typeof." Since JavaScript is dynamically typed, at various point in the program we need to know which type of data the variable contains. We can determine that using typeof operator.

# typeof Operator

Like I mentioned before, typeof operator is used to determining the type of data a variable is holding. For example

```
typeof "Amit"              // "string"
typeof ""                  // "string" (empty string)
typeof 314                 // "number"
typeof 3.14                // "number"
typeof (3 + 4)             // "number"
typeof false               // "boolean"
typeof [1,2,3,4]           // "object"because arrays are
considered as object in JavaScript
typeof {name:'Amit', age:70}       // "object"
```

Now that I have explained typeof operator let us look at what exactly is the difference between undefined and null.If we operate typeof on null, it returns an object whereas if we operate typeof on undefined, undefined is returned.

# Constants

Constant as the name suggests are those variables whose value cannot be changed. These are declared using const Keyword and must be assigned a value during the time of declaration. It can either be local to a function or can be a global variable. Constants once assigned cannot be changed. Their value remains read-only throughout the program. For example:

const pi= 3.14;                    //Declaring and initializing a constant


This chapter explained variables, data types, and constants. I hope you enjoyed reading it and found it helpful.

CHAPTER 8

# BASIC OPERATORS

## What are operators?

Operators are basically symbols which act as a function, though they differ from functions syntax-wise. They take input(operands) and produce a certain output based on the operands. For example in "5+2", "5" and "2" are operands(the input), and the "+" symbol is the operator, which results to "7".

## Classification of operators

Operators are generally classified on the basis of the type of operation they do. Operators like typeof, instanceof, etc. are unique and thus cannot be classified under the categories about which you will read below.

# Arithmetic Operators

As the name hints, these are the operators which perform arithmetic tasks on the operand(s). Listed below are the arithmetic operators.

- Addition[+]: This operator performs an addition operation on two operands if both of them are numerical, if anyone or both of the two operands are of string type then this operator concatenates / joins the two operands.
  Example:

  | | |
  |---|---|
  | 4 + 2 | //evaluates to 6 |
  | 'example' + 5 | //evaluates to "example5" |
  | 'thisIs' + 'Example' | //evaluates to "thisIsExample". |

- Subtraction[-]: This operator performs a subtraction operation on two operands. Example: "4-2" produces the result "2".

- Division[/]: This operator performs division operation on two operands, where the operand on left side(dividend) is divided by the operand on the right side(divisor). Example: "15/3" produces the result "3".

- Multiplication[*]: This operator performs multiplication operation on two operands. Example: "4*2" produces the result "8".

- Modulus[%]: Also known as a Remainder operator, this operator results in the remainder of the two operands when they are divided. Example: "5%2" produces the result "1", "5%3" produces the result "2".

- Increment[++]: Increases the value of its numerical operand by one. The position of this operator matters, i.e., whether it is placed before operand or after it. If placed before operand, then this situation is called prefix(example ++x), and the value is returned after the incrementing operation, and if placed after the operand then this situation is called postfix(example x++), and value is returned before the incrementing operation.

Example:

```
//say x value is 5
console.log( ++x ); //prints 6
//value of x at this point is 6


//say y value is 5 too
```

console.log( y++ ); //prints 5 NOT 6
//but value of y at this point is 6 so incrementation
was done but after the expression returned value

- Decrement[--]: Decreases the value of its numerical
operand by one. Similar to increment operator, the
postfix and prefix rule applies here too.
Example:

//say x value is 5
console.log( --x ); //prints 4
// value of x at this point is 4

//say y value is 5 too
console.log( y-- ); //prints 5
//value of y at this point is 4

- Exponential[**]: This operator produces the result
obtained by increasing the first operand power by the
second operand, i.e., FirstOperand$^{SecondOperand}$.
Example: "2**3" produces the result "8".

# Assignment Operators

These operators are used to assign values to variables.
Value is assigned to the left operand which is based on

the right operand value. Listed below are the assignment operators.

- Equal[=]: This operator simply assigns the value of its right operand to the left operand. Example: "x=5" this assigns 5 to x, so now the value of x is 5.

- Addition assignment[+=]: This operator adds the value of the left and the right operand and then assigns the result to the left operand. Example: say x = 2 then "x += 3" will make x's value 5.

- Subtraction assignment[-=]: This operator subtracts the value of the right operand from the left operand and then assigns the result to the left operand. Example: say x = 8 then "x -= 3" will make x's value 5.

- Multiplication assignment[*=]: This operator multiplies the left and the right operand and assigns the result to the left operand. Example: say x = 5 then "x *= 2" will make x's value 10.

- Division Assignment[/=]: This operator divides the left operand(dividend) by the right operand(divisor) and then assigns the result to the left operand.

Example: say x = 10 then "x /= 2" will make x's value 5.

- Modulus Assignment[%=]: This operator divides the left operand(dividend) by the right operand(divisor) and then assigns the REMAINDER to the left operand. Example: say x = 5 then "x %= 2" will make x's value 1.

- Exponentiation assignment: This operator increases the value of left operand by the power of right operand and then assigns the result produced to the left operand. Example: say x = 2 then "x **= 3" will make x's value 8.

## Other Operators

These are the type of operators which cannot be categorized under the above-mentioned categories. Listed below are such operators.

- typeof operator: This operator returns the type of operand in string format. Examples:

```
typeof 2            //evaluates to "number"
typeof 1.23         //evaluates to "number"
```

```
typeof "2"          //evaluates to "string"
typeof 'hi'         //evaluates to "string"

typeof true              //evaluates to "boolean"
typeof false             //evaluates to "boolean"

typeof {ob:1}            //evaluates to "object"
typeof new Date()        //evaluates to "object"

tyepof Math.cos   //evaluates to "function"
typeof function(){}      //evaluates to "function"
```

- instanceof operator: This operator checks if the first operand, which should be an object, is of a specific type, where the type to be checked is specified as the second operand. It returns true or false based on whether the object type is matched or not.
  Examples:

```
new String("Astring") instanceof String
     //evaluates to true
["this", "is", "array"] instanceof Array
     //evaluates to true
```

new String("Astring") instance of Array
//evaluates to false
["this", "is", "array"] instanceof String   //evaluates to false

- delete operator: This operator removes a property from an object. Example:

```
var myObject = {
    prop1: "test",
    prop2: "test2"
};
```

```
delete myObject.prop1;  //deletes the prop1 property of object myObject
```

- in operator: This operator checks whether a specified property(first operand) is in the specified object(second operand). It returns true or false based on whether the property is in the object or not. Examples:

```
var myObject = {
    prop1: "test",
    prop2: "test2"
```

```
};
```

```
"prop1" in myObject;        //evaluates to true
```

```
"prop45" in myObject;       //evaluates to false
```

This chapter explained operators in JavaScript. I hope you found it useful.

# CHAPTER 9

# FUNCTIONS IN JAVASCRIPT

Functions form an integral part of any programming language. If not for the functions, our program would contain lots of redundant code. Function helps us write code in an efficient manner which not only improves the readability but also contribute a great deal while maintaining it. Let us explore what a function is and why it is required!

A function is a set of statements which are used to carry out a particular task. It is as simple as saying that you have a function which carries out the addition of two numbers. So at any point in the program, if you need to calculate the sum of two numbers, you just call this particular function and pass the two values to be added. The function will then return the desired value. Let us first look at the syntax for declaring and defining a function and then we will discuss in detail about it.

```
function          functionName(parameter1,          parameter2,
parameter3) {
    //set of statements to be executed
}
```

As you can see above, a function definition starts with the
keyword "function," followed by a unique function
name, followed by a parenthesis ( ). The task which the
function is supposed to execute is written curly braces.
So whenever a function is called, all the statements
within the curly braces will be executed. If you notice in
the above syntax, there are a set of parameters within the
parenthesis which are separated by commas. These are
the values which the function requires in order to
produce the desired result. Or in other words, these are
the values one must pass while calling the function.

Let us look at a simple example of a function which
accepts two values and return their sum.

```
function addTwoNumbers(num1, num2){

        return num1+num2; //Calculates and returns the
sum
}
```

One must note that a function remains dormant or inactive until and unless it is invoked or called in the main program. Consider these analogous to a toast maker present in the kitchen. Toast maker is supposed to toast a bread which you supply to it. It remains inactive unless you need it. When you need it, you just put the bread inside and switch it on. It then does the usual. Same happens with a function too. It is executed when it is called or invoked.

Each function should have its own unique function name. This is important because when you call a function, there should be no ambiguous situation.

The parameters behave as local variables inside the function. If you have knowledge about some other programming languages, you might have heard of procedure or subroutine. What is subroutine to them is a function in JavaScript.

A function is executed when it is invoked. This can happen because of one of the following scenarios:

- When it is called from a JavaScript program.
- Automatically invoked.

- When some events occur (Events generally refers to an activity which happens on the web page)

Whenever a return statement is encountered, the value is returned to the place where it is called from. Any statement beyond the return statement in the function is not executed. Therefore it is extremely important that the return statement is placed at the end of the function. In some cases, we might have to place the return in the beginning, but then again that will happen in the case of conditional statements.

Let us look at another example which calculates the product of two numbers. This will help us in understanding the concept of function call in a better way.

```
function productCalc(num1, num2) {
    return num1 * num2 ; //Product calculated &returned
}

var prod = productCalc(5, 6);
```

In the above example, the productCalc function is called, and the returned value is stored in the value prod. You can then chose to use the value wherever required.

Now that we have seen what function is and how to use them according to our need let us look at why the function is very important in today's world of efficient programming.

Advantages of functions:

## 1. Reusability

The main advantage of a function is the fact that it can be reused throughout the program. You can write a function which performs a certain task and then simply call it whenever you are required to perform that task. For example, If you have to sort some numbers, you can write a function which does that and then no matter how many times you are required to sort some numbers, you can just call the function, and your job will be done. You escape from writing the same code for sorting again and again.

## 2. Maintainability

Maintainability refers to the task of refactoring a piece of code at a later point in the time. Let us say, the code you wrote to sort a list of numbers has a bug. Now imagine you don't have the concept of functions. So basically wherever you have used that buggy code, you need to search it and then rectify a bug. With function, however, you just look at one place and correct the code. You need not visit several places. This saves you a lot of time and effort.

## 3. Reduced code length

With function in place, you don't need to write the same set of codes everywhere. This reduces the length of the code significantly.

Few points to remember about function

1. You can use document.getElementById() to show the result of function anywhere in the HTML page.

   For example:

   ```
   function add(a,b) {
               return a+b;
   }

   document.getElementById("result").innerHTML
   = add(7,14);
   ```

2. Always use the () operator to invoke a function. In case you miss, the whole text of the function is returned.

In the previous example, if you simply call add instead of add(), the HTML will contain the whole function text.

3. The function can be directly used as the value of a variable.

For example:

var x = add(5,7);
var printString = "The result is " + x ;

Or,

var printString= "The result is " + add(5,7);

In both the cases, the output will be same.

Always remember if you write a set of code which is repeating several times throughout the program, create a function out of it. Also, the length of the function should be kept as small as possible.

# CHAPTER 10

# UNDERSTANDING OBJECTS

JavaScript is based on the paradigm of OOP(Object Oriented Programming) hence almost everything in it is an object or at least behaves like one, be it an array, function or regular expression(regex). An object is the most fundamental block of JavaScript.

## What are objects?

An object is a collection of properties and has a type. Just as in other programming languages, one can understand the concept of an object by comparing it to real-life objects. Let's take a car, for example, the same model car may have a different color, i.e., have different properties, but it belongs to the same category which is a car, i.e., it is of the same type.

Here is an example for understanding the object's concept as described above more clearly:

```
function cars(color, numberPlate) {
    //this is like blueprint of object, not the object it self
    this.color = color;
    this.numberPlate = numberPlate;
}
//Creating Objects:
var car1 = new car("Green", 1234);//they are of same type
var car2 = new car("Red", 5678);//but have different
properties

console.log(car1);//outputs car1 details, i.e., Green and
1234 on console
console.log(car2);//outputs car2 details, i.e., Red and 5678
on console
```

## Accessing object's properties

In JavaScript, you can access the object properties in two ways, viz, the dot notation and the bracket notation. The syntax of both ways are as follows:

```
myObject.propertyName;      //dot notation
```

```
myObject['propertyName'];   //bracket notation
```

Note that if the object property is integral, then it can be accessed only with bracket notation, example:

```
myObject.55        //WRONG
myObject['55'];    //RIGHT
```

# Creating objects In JavaScript

Listed below are the ways to create objects in JavaScript:

- **Object Literal:**

This is the most common and probably the easiest way of creating an object in JavaScript.

Example:

```
var myObject = {
    objectProperty1: 45,
    objectProperty2: 'something else',
    objectMethod: function() {//using function as object
property
        console.log(this.objectProperty1,
```

this.objectProperty2);//prints object property on console
```
  }
};
```

myObject.objectMethod();//example call to object method/function


- **Using the 'new' keyword:**

You can create objects by calling the object constructor(a function used to initialize new objects) with 'new' keyword.

Example:

```
var myObject = new Object();//constructor to initialize new object
myObject.property1 = 45;
myObject.property2 = 'something else';
myObject.objectMethod = function() { /* ... */ };
```

You can also define your own constructor function to create new objects; the constructor function is like a blueprint of your object, you can create many objects ensuring that they are all of the same types, though they may have different properties.

Example of custom constructor function:

```
function students(name, age, class) {
    this.name = name;
this.age = age;
this.class = class
}
//using 'new' keyword to create object from custom constructor function:
var student1 = new student("Sam", 14, 2);//a student with name sam and age 17 of class 2
var student2 = new student("Joe", 17, 11);//a student of age 17 and class 11
```

## Nested objects

You can create an object within an object. This can be done by assigning an object to an object's property. This is called nesting.

Example:

```
var student = {
    name: "Mark",
    marks : { //nesting
        maths: 80,
        english: 95
    }
};
//nested objects can be referenced like this:
student.marks.maths;        // dot notation
student['marks']['maths']   // bracket notation
```

## Use of 'this' keyword In objects

The keyword 'this' inside an object references the object in which it is being used. It is used to access or assign values to the object properties from within itself.

Example:

```
function objectConstructor(value) {
this.objectProperty = value;     //assigning new value to
our object
console.log( this.objectProperty ); //accessing our
object's property
}
```

# Objects are reference data types

Primitive data types are referenced by their values whereas reference data types are referenced by their address.

Understanding the difference with an example:

```
// Primitive data types:
var x = 45;
var y = x;
x = 10;
console.log(x);   // 10
console.log(y);   // 45
```

As you can see in the above example, altering the value of 'x' didn't have any effect on value of 'y', but it is not the same with reference data types, let's see the same type of example with reference data types:

```
var x = { value: 45 };// object, reference data type
var y = x;
x.value = 10;
console.log(x.value);// 10
console.log(y.value);// 10
```

As illustrated in the above example, altering the value of 'x' this time affected the value of 'y', this is because object being a reference data type, is being referenced by address so the same address gets assigned to 'y' and any change in that brings about change to both 'x' and 'y'. This is why objects in JavaScript are said to be Mutable, meaning changeable.

# Removing an object's property

As studied in chapter 5, we can use the 'delete' operator to delete an object's property. To delete a property from an object, you have to write the 'delete' operator followed by the object with its property to be deleted.

Example:

```
var student = {
    name:'Joe',
    age: 16
};
console.log(student.age);//16
delete student.age;//deleting the property
console.log( student.age ); //gives an error saying 'undefined'
```

# Looping through object's properties

You can loop through object's properties with the help of for-in loop.

Example:

```
var carList = {
    car1: 'Mustang',
    car2: 'Beetle',
    car3: 'Viper'
};
//looping thorugh object's properties:
for(var property in carList) {
    console.log( property ); //outputs Mustang, Beetle,
Viper
}
```

An alternative to loop through object's properties is to use the Object.key() method of the Object class to obtain an array of keys and then loop through that array to access the properties of objects.

Example:

```
//using the same object as the example above
for (const propertyName of Object.keys(carList)) {
  console.log(carList[propertyName]);
}
```

You have learned how to work with objects in JavaScript.
I hope you have found this chapter useful!

# CHAPTER 11

# SCOPE OF A VARIABLE

Variables are created in JavaScript to act as containers to store data. Unlike other compiled languages like C/C++ where it is mandatory to define the type of data to be stored explicitly, JavaScript makes no such divisions and stores every type of data like string, integers, floating point integers, Boolean, etc. by the same constructor *var*.

var x=2;
var y=0.04;
z='A';

All these are variables have a scope and a lifetime which is the time that the value that they contain will be valid.

# Scope

Let's talk about the scope of a variable, first. JavaScript has two scopes:

- Global
- Local

If we say that a variable has global scope, it means that the variable can be used throughout the script, in all functions that are within the script. It can be accessed, modified everywhere. While in the case of a variable that has local scope, they can be accessed or modified only within the function within which they have been defined.

A variable that is declared inside a function is a Local variable. It is only created when the function is executed, stays alive till the function is running and then gets destroyed automatically. The variable cannot be accessed anywhere outside that function.

```
varmyVar= "Something";
functionmyFunc(){
varmyVar= "Another thing";
}
```

As can be seen, we can have a local as well as a global variable of the same name. The difference occurs at the place at which they're being called.

For example, if we print the value of the variable myVarinside the function, we'd get "Another thing" printed on the screen. On the other hand, if we try to print the value of myVar outside that function, we'd get "Something" printed on the display. So we can see it's just the placement of the variable that decides entirely whether it's a local or a global variable.

When JavaScript starts to execute a function, it first looks for all the variable declarations that exist inside the function, for example, var foo. Then it creates all the variables with the initial value undefined. If the variable is declared along with some value inside the function, it still is initialized with the value undefined. Then, JavaScript starts to execute the present statements line by line. When it reaches the line where the variable declaration is made, it gives that variable that value, removing the undefined label.

Example:

```
var something=100;
foo();
function foo(){
console.log(something);
if(false)
var something=112;
}
```

The console.log here will print undefined. The reason is that when the function is executed, the variable that is declared inside that if statement is taken and the value is set to be undefined. Then that console.log statement occurs.

Had the if statement not there, we would have got 100 printed on the console.

# Closures

In JavaScript, the nested function stores references to the variable declared in the same scope as the function. This set of references is called *Closures*.

Example:

```
function foo(name){
        return function(){
bar(name);
        }
}
function bar(name){
console.log("Hello"+name);
}
```

When the function is called with something like, foo("John") the console.log will display Hello John on the display.

How's this happening? Go through that code snippet once again. The foo() function makes a call to the function bar() whose signature has an argument with it. When foo() is called, the inner nested function gets the reference to the argument of foo() in this case which is "John." This reference to the variable that the nested function bar() got is a closure in JavaScript. That is how closures work.

# ES6 specification

ECMA script is the super class of JavaScript and acts like a standard for the language. JavaScript has added features in the 2015 version of the script which includes the introduction of block-scoped variables, let and const. For these variables {..} defines a new scope. When the variable like them are initialized, it only affects the scope in which they're defined in.

Example:

```
let a=2;
const b=3;
{
let a=3;
console.log(a);
}
console.log(a);
```

Both these console.log() statements will print different values. The reason being that both the variables "a" have been defined in different scopes.

# Conclusion

JavaScript variables are the easiest to work with as they involve no type setting as is the case with other compiled language, and hence is called weakly-typed. It offers us so many functionalities that we can use. The language keeps on enhancing and since 2015 has added the let and const variables that make the life of a JavaScript programmer easier and interesting.

# CHAPTER 12

# WORKING WITH NUMBERS IN JAVASCRIPT

Most of the programming involves working with numbers. Whether it is working with the balance in a bank account, or sending encrypted messages across to other users, or nearly anything else, you will be performing arithmetic operations, trying to find square roots and so on, or finding random numbers to use. Javascript makes these tasks a lot simpler than many other languages, and most of these operations are very intuitive.

## How JavaScript stores numbers

Before we get started on how to work with numbers, learning how exactly Javascript sees them is necessary. Javascript (JS) stores all numbers as floating point numbers - that is, all numbers can have decimal points.

Unlike most C style languages, there is no separate type for integers. All numbers are stored in the Number type. You can store use numbers as follows:

var x = 12;
var y = 2.66;
var z = 312e-2;

The last example is a case of using exponential notation. In this case, z is equal to 3.12. In many cases, if you have a number in a string, JS will try to convert it to a number for numeric calculations. For example,

var num = "1234";

If you try to use num in numerical operations, it is treated as 1234. However, there is one very important quirk to this during addition, which we will see shortly.

Arithmetic operations

First, let's look at how to perform basic arithmetic operations. These include addition, subtraction, multiplication, and division. These are done as follows:

```
        var x = 12 + 24;
```
X will now store the value 36.
```
        var x = 24 / 2;
```
X will now store the value 12.
```
        var x = 3 - 2;
```
X will store the value 1.
```
        var x = 4 * 9;
```
X will store the value 36.

Note that all of these will work with using strings as numbers, as well, except for the addition operator +. Let's take a look at a few statements:

```
var x = 24 / "2";
var y = "3" * "4";
var z = "12" + 3;
var n = 36 / "Mike";
```

The first will result in 12, as expected, and so will the next. But, z will hold the value "123" and *not* 15. This is because the + operator is performing *concatenation* - it is joining two strings together. In this case, JS converted 3 to "3" and then added those two strings together to get "123". You will have to keep this in mind every time you are adding anything that could be a string!

The last one is also interesting. There is no obvious answer to this - 36 can't be divided by Mike. JS fills n with the value NaN - short for Not a Number. Every time you perform a numeric computation that can't result in a number, you will get a NaN as the result. If you want to check if a variable is a NaN, you can do this:

isNaN(n);

This will return true! You can also fill a variable with NaN yourself. Similarly, when you perform a calculation that results in infinity, JS will return the value Infinity.

var p = 12 / 0;

The variable p will have the value Infinity. Infinity is not the string "Infinity," it's a value.

## Using built-in functions

For simple things like getting a number down to a certain number of decimal places, or converting it to a string, JS has built-in functions. Most of these functions are used by the syntax object.method(arguments);

To convert a number to a string, you can use the toString() method:

```
    var x = 25;
var x_in_string = x.toString;
```

x_in_string will be equal to "25". The toExponential(n) method writes the number out in scientific notation, with n digits behind the decimal point. The argument n is optional, and you can replace it with any number.

```
    var x = 25.321;
    var x_in_exponents = x.toExponent(3);
```

x_in_exponents will be "25.321e0". Note that the output is a string. If you call toExponent() without an argument, it will not round the number at all. The toFixed(n) method works to output the number with a certain number of decimal places.

```
    var x = 25.1168;
    var x_to_2 = x.toFixed(2);
```

x_to_2 will be "25.12". Note that it rounds the number. Often you will need to convert a string into a number. THis may be especially useful in the case we saw above where you tried to add a string and a number. To prevent concatenation, you should use the function Number(). This function is used differently:

```
var x = "25.12";
var y = Number(x);
```

Now y will have the value 25. There are two more functions you can use: parseInt() and parseFloat(). These two functions take the first number in the string and return it rounded and as with the decimal respectively.

```
var x = "10.2 20 30";
var y = parseInt(x);
var z = parseFloat(x);
```

y will be 10 and x will be 10.2. All of these functions will return a NaN if the number cannot be converted.

## The Math functions

Arithmetic operators don't cover all you need to do with numbers. To do things like finding the square root or the absolute value of a number, you have to use the Math functions. These are generally used by the syntax Math.method(argument).

The first set of functions are Math.round(), Math.ceil(), and Math.floor(). The Math.round() function rounds a number to an integer. If the first digit after the decimal place is greater than or equal to 5, it rounds up to the next integer, and if it is less than 5, it rounds down to the previous integer. The ceil function is similar except it always rounds a number up to the next integer, and the floor function always rounds it down to the previous integer.

```
var x = 25.52;
var y = 25.19;
var xRound = Math.round(x);
var yRound = Math.round(y);
var xCeil = Math.ceil(x);
var yCeil = Math.ceil(y);
var xFloor = Math.floor(x);
var yFloor = Math.floor(y);
```

xRound will be 26 and yRound 25. xCeil and yCeil will both be 26, and xFloor and yFloor will both be 25. The Math.pow() function can be used to find a number raised to the power of another number. For example:

```
var x = Math.pow(2,10);
```

x will be 1024. Finding the square root, or the power of ½, is a very common operation, which you can perform using Math.sqrt():

```
var x = Math.sqrt(9);
```

And x will be 3. The Math.abs() function returns the absolute value of a number passed to it.

```
var x = Math.abs(-2);
```

X will be 2. The Math.min() and Math.max() functions can be used to find the minimum and maximum of a list of numbers given to them. They can take any number of arguments.

```
var maximum = Math.max(10,12,14,3,7,1,3);
var minimum = Math.min(10,12,14,3,7,1,3);
```

Maximum will take the value 14 and minimum will take the value 1. The math library also has built in functions for trigonometric functions like sin, cos and tan, and their inverses. These functions are Math.sin(), Math.cos(), Math.tan(), Math.asin(), Math.acos(), Math.atan(). All of these functions work in radians, so you should convert any angles in degrees to radians for use.

```
var sinpi = Math.sin(Math.PI);
```

Sinpi will take the value 0. Finally, the Math.log() function allows you find the natural logarithm of a number.

```
var logten = Math.log(10);
```

logten will take the value 2.302. JS also has a few mathematical constants, such as Pi and E, in the Math library.

# Random numbers

For cases like cryptography and video games, random numbers are very important. To generate random numbers, you can use the Math.random() function. The Math.random() function returns a random number between 0 and 1, 1 exclusive and 0 inclusive.

```
var n = Math.random();
```

N will take a different value every time. To make use of this in situations where you need a random number between two numbers a and b, you can use the following code:

```
var randn = a + (Math.random() * (a-b));
```

This will always give you a number between a and b. To get an integer between a and b, you can use the floor, ceil or round functions we saw up above.

# CHAPTER 13

# WORKING WITH STRINGS IN JAVASCRIPT

Strings are a group of characters. It stores a series of characters. As specified in previous chapters, we use single or double quotes for storing a string. For example:

```
var name= "Amit"; //Double quotes
Or,
var name= 'Amit'; //Single Quotes
```

What if the string itself contains single or double quotes? For example:

```
var desc= "He is referred as the "Don" among his colleagues"; //Error
Or
var desc = 'It's alright';        //Error
```

In those cases, we make use of escape character ( \ ) to demarcate our string in a proper manner. The escape character specifies to the compiler that there are special characters following that. Let us understand this better with an example.

var desc= "He is referred to as the \"Don\" among his colleagues";

Or,

var desc = 'It\'s alright';        //Error


Sometimes we can also use a simple way. If the string contains double quotes, then enclose the entire string in a single quote and if the string contains single quotes, then enclose the entire string in double quote. For example:

var answer = "It's alright";
var desc= 'He is referred to as the "Don"among his colleagues';

Escape characters can also be used for some other special characters like a backslash (\), backspace (\b), carriage return (\r), etc.

Every string has a built-in property known as the length which can be used to know the length of a string. For example:

```
var textRand = "INDIA";
var len= textRand.length; //len will store 5
```

Sometimes it might happen that the string is longer than usual. In those cases, the string might not fit in a single line. That often can result in confusion. To prevent this from creating confusions and causing problems, we divide the string into two parts and then concatenate it using a plus (+) operator. For example:

```
var longTxt= "ABCB CBCB BBBB BBBB BBBB BBBB
BBBB BBB BBCB CB CCBC" +
"AN ADDITION TO A REALLY LONG TEXT";
```

One interesting fact about JavaScript String is that they can act as primitive values as well as can be defined as objects. Let us understand this through an example.

```
var text= "Hello";
var text1= new String("Hello");
```

If we try to determine the type of both the variables using the typeof operator, we will get different results.

Typeof(text) will return string whereas typeof(text1) will return an object. However, it must be noted that creating strings as objects is not a good practice. This is because creating strings as objects slows down the execution speed.

Sometimes we need to check the equality of two strings. There are two ways to do so. One of the ways is to use "==" operator, which just checks whether those two strings have equal values. The other way is to use "===" operator, which not only compares their values but also checks their types. For example:

```
var text= "Hello";
var text1= new String("Hello");
```

```
//If we execute text==text1, the output will be true since
the value of both the strings is equal.
```

//However, If we execute text===text1, the output is false. This is because the text is a normal string while text1 is an object.

//In case both the strings to be compared are objects, === will return false because both the string are treated as different objects.

We should not treat the string as arrays. Writing name[1] will not provide any error, but this might not always work. Some browsers like internet explorer do not support this. In order to avoid this, one must always convert the string to arrays. The conversion of a string to an array can be done using the split() method. This splits the string to arrays using a separator. For example:

```
var name = "a,m,i,t";
name.split(",");        // commas
name.split(" ");        // spaces
```

//In case the separator is omitted, the resultant array will contain //the whole string at index[0] )
In case the separator is the resultant array will consist of single characters. For example:
var intro = "My name is Amit";

intro.split("");        // The string is split in characters.

There are several methods and various properties associated with strings which make some operations on the string very easy. Let us look at them one by one.

## 1. The Length property

Every string has a length property associated with them. It returns the number of characters the string has.

For example:

var randText="ABC DEF GHI";
var len= randText.length;        //len will contain 11

## 2. The indexOf() method

This method returns the position (index) of the first occurrence of a specified text in the string. It returns -1 if the given string is not found. The index starts from 0.

For example:

var text = "My name is Amit";
var ind = text.indexOf("Amit");
//This will return 11 because Amit is present at location 11

## 3. The lastIndexOf() method

This method returns the position (index) of the last occurrence of the given text in the string. It returns -1 if the given string is not found.

var str = "Our own planet earth is a great planet";
var n = str.lastIndexOf("planet");
//This will return 31 as last occurrence of planet is at 31

Note: Both of the above methods accept the2nd parameter as well which the position is from where the search has to start.

var text = "My name is Amit";
var ind = text.indexOf("Amit",2);
//In this case, the search starts from index 2

## 4. The search() method

The search method behaves exactly same as the indexOf() method. However, it does not accept any second parameter. Therefore, in this case, the search starts from index 0 in all the cases. This is used for searching a pattern of strings using regular expressions.

### 5. The slice() method

The slice() method takes two parameters – start and end. As the name suggests, slice returns the string from start index to end index.

For example:

```
var country = "India, Bahama, Fiji";
var res = country.slice(7, 13);

//This will return Bahama

// In case the second parameter is omitted, rest of the string is chopped off.

//In case the index is negative, it counts from end
```

**6.** The substring() method

The substring() method is similar to slice() except that substring() cannot accept negative indexes.

    var country = "India, Bahama, Fiji";
    var res = country.substring(7, 13);

//This will return Bahama

// In case the second parameter is omitted, rest of the string is chopped off.

**7.** The substr() Method

This method again is similar to slice() except that the two parameters which this method accepts are start index and length of the extracted part. For example:

    var country = "India, Bahama, Fiji";
    var res = country.substr(7, 13);

//This will return Bahama

// In case the second parameter is omitted, rest of the string is chopped off.

**8.** The replace() method

This method works exactly like find and replace. This replaces the given value with some other value in the string, both of which has to be passed as parameters.

name    =    "My    name    is    Amit";
var n = name.replace("Amit", "Amitabh");

However, the thing to note is that the original string remains unaffected. A new string is returned. By default, It only replaces the first match of the string.

In order to replace all the matches in the string, we use a regular expression with /g flag which means replace all the global matches.

name = "My name is Amit and Amit";
var n = name. replace("/Amit/g", "Amitabh");

The replace function is case sensitive by default. To make it case insensitive, we use /i. For example:

name = "My name is Amit and Amit";
var n = name. replace ("/Amit/i", "Amitabh"

9.  The toUppercase() method

96

No prize for guessing! This function converts a string to uppercase. For example:

```
var text1 = "Amit";
var text2 = text1.toUpperCase();  //returns AMIT
```

## 10. The toLowerCase() method

No prize for guessing! This function converts a string to lowercase. For example:

```
var text1 = "Amit";
var text2 = text1.toLowerCase();  //returns amit
```

## 11. The concat() method

This method is used to join two or strings.
For example:

```
var text1 = "Name is";
var text2 = "Amit";
var text3 = text1.concat(" ", text2);
```

```
//Result will be "Name is Amit"
```

## 12. The charAt( ) method

This method is used to extract a character from a specified position. For example:

```
var name="Amitabh";
name.charAt(1); // This will return "m"
```

### 13. The charCodeAt( ) method

This method is used to determine the Unicode of the character at a specified location. For example:

```
var name = "Himalaya";
name.charCodeAt(0);      // returns 72
```

To be honest, we deal with strings the most in the case of JavaScript. So it is necessary that you understand it to the core. Most of the time you will encounter strings, therefore understand its practical uses. The methods associated with strings can be considered as weapons which should be used as per the requirement. There are several other methods of JavaScript strings. You can search them online.

# CHAPTER 14

# WORKING WITH DATE AND TIME IN JAVASCRIPT

Date and time manipulation is an important part of JavaScript, being a developer you will be facing situations where date and time will play a crucial role.

## The 'Date' object

In JavaScript, we use the inbuilt 'Date' object to manipulate date and time; it provides with many useful functions for efficient date and time manipulation.

## Initializing the 'Date' object

You can initialize a new date object with the help of the 'new' operator in JavaScript. There are four formats in which you can initialize the date object, which are listed below.

- new Date()

  When initialized without any argument, the date object points to current date and time.

  Example :

  ```
  var example = new Date();
  console.log( example ); //shows current date and time
  ```

  The resulting date and time are relative to the local timezone of the system on which the code is run.

- new Date(milliseconds)

  When initialized with a single argument which is an integer, that integer is taken as millisecond(one second equals $10^3$ milliseconds) and the date object thus formed points to the date and time which you get by adding the specified number of milliseconds added to Jan 1st of 1970 UTC+0. These milliseconds passed since Jan 1st of 1970 UTC+0 used to specify date and time is called timestamp.

  Example:

  ```
  car example = new Date (24 * 3600 * 1000); //adding one day
  console.log( example ); // Fri Jan 02 1970 ...
  ```

- new Date(datestring)

  If the date object is initialized with a single argument which is a string, then it is taken as a date string (you will read about valid date strings later in this chapter), and the date object thus created points to the date and time specified in date string.

  Example:

  var date = new Date("2017-01-26");
  alert(date); // Thu Jan 26 2017 ...

- new Date(year, month [,date, hours, minutes, seconds, ms])

  If initialized with the format mentioned above then the newly created date object will point to that date time. Please note that only the first two arguments are mandatory when initializing the date like this rest are set to zero by default if not specified.

  Example:

new Date(2011, 0, 1, 0, 25, 12, 0); // 1 Jan 2011, 25:12:00

new Date(2011, 0, 1); // 1 Jan 2011, 00:00:00

## Valid Date strings

Date strings are the strings which contain a date in the string format, here are the valid formats for date string in JavaScript:

- YYYY-MM-DD
  This is ISO date format which is the International standard way for the representation of dates.
  Example: "2017-07-17"

- YYYY-MM
  You can also write ISO date without specifying the day; the day will be set to the first day of the month by default.
  Example: "07/17/2017."

- YYYY

You can also just write the year; this will make the date 1st of Jan of that year, i.e., the first day of the year.
Example: "2017."

- MMM DD YYYY or DD MMM YYYY
MMM stands for abbreviated month name.For example, the abbreviated form of July is 'Jul'.
Example: "Jul17 2017" or "17Jul 2017."
You can also write the non-abbreviated form of the month, i.e., the full name of the month.
Example: "July 17 2017."

- MM/DD/YYYY
This format is also known as short date representation of a date.
Example: "07/17/2017."

- YYYY-MM-DDTHH:MM:SSZ
In this format, the character 'T' is just for separating date with time and the Z tells JavaScript that we are specifying the date with respect to UTC(Universal Time Coordinated).
Example: "2017-07-17T10:00:00Z"

You can also specify date and time with respect to other time zones by replacing the Z with +HH:MM or -HH:MM.

Example: "2017-07-17T10:00:00+05:30"

# Getting components from the Date object

You can use the methods provided by the date object to access specific components(year, day, month, etc.) of the date object. Generally, the name of these type of methods begins with 'get'. Here are the methods:

- getFullYear()

    This method returns the four digit year of the date.

    Example:

    ```
    var myDate = new Date("2017-07-17");
    console.log( myDate.getFullYear() ); // 2017
    ```

- getDate()

This method returns the day of the month as a number. Possible return values of this method ranges from 1 – 31.
Example:

```
var myDate = new Date("2017-07-17");
console.log( myDate.getDate() ); // 17
```

- getMonth()

  This method returns the month as an integer. Please note that this method returns values from 0 – 11 not from 1 – 12 as you would expect, where 0 represents first month, i.e., January.
  Example:

```
var myDate = new Date("2017-07-17");
console.log( myDate.getMonth() ); // 6
```

- getDay()

  This method returns the day of the week as an integer.

Example:

```
var myDate = new Date("2017-07-17");
console.log( myDate.getDay() ); // 1 – which is
monday
```

- getHours()
  This method returns the hour of the day as an
  integer, possible return values ranges from 0 – 23.
  Example:

```
var myDate = new Date("2017-07-17T10:21:35Z");
console.log( myDate.getHours() ); // 10
```

- getMinutes()
  This method returns the minute of the hour as an
  integer, possible return values ranges from 0 – 59.
  Example:

```
var myDate = new Date("2017-07-17T10:21:35Z");
console.log( myDate.getMinutes() ); // 21
```

- getSeconds()
  This method returns the second of the minute as
  an integer, possible return values ranges from 0 –
  59.

Example:

```
var myDate = new Date("2017-07-17T10:21:35Z");
console.log( myDate.getSeconds() ); // 35
```

- getTime()
  This method returns the date and time as number of milliseconds passed since since January 1, 1970. Example:

```
var myDate = new Date("2017-07-17T10:21:35Z");
console.log(    myDate.getTime()    );    //
1500286895000
```

Note that the above-mentioned method returns the component of the date relative to the local time zone, if you want them with respect to UTC you can just add the word "UTC" after the "get" part of the method in the above-mentioned methods, for example, "getHours()" becomes "getUTCHours()".

# Setting components of the Date object

The date object also provides us for setting date components! Generally, the name of these methods begins with "set". Here are the methods:

- setFullYear(year [, month, date])
  This method is used to set the date to a specific date, only the first argument in this method is mandatory.

  Example:

  ```
  var myDate = new Date();
  myDate.setFullYear(2017, 6, 17);
  ```

- setMonth(month [, date])
  This method is used to set the date to a specific month of the year; you can also set the day of the month, which is optional. The integer 0 represents the first month, i.e., January and 11 represents the last.
  Example:

  ```
  var myDate = new Date();
  myDate.setMonth( 6); //set month to july
  ```

- setDate(date)
  This method is used to set the day of the month, where 1 represents first day of the month.
  Example:

  ```
  var myDate = new Date();
  ```

myDate.setDate( 17 );

- setHours(hour [, min, sec, ms])
This method is used to set the time of the date object, only the first argument in this method is mandatory.
Example:

var myDate = new Date();
myDate.setHours( 11 );

- setMinutes(min [, sec, ms])
This method is used to set the minute of the hour, you can also set second and millisecond using this method, but those are optional.
Example:

var myDate = new Date();
myDate.setMinutes( 20 );

- setSeconds(sec, [, ms])
This method is used to set the second of the minute, you can also set the millisecond using this method but that is optional.
Example:

```
var myDate = new Date();

myDate.setSeconds( 58 );
```

- setMilliseconds(ms)
  This method is used to set the millisecond of the
  second.
  Example:

```
var myDate = new Date();

myDate.setMilliseconds( 123 );
```

- setTime(milliseconds)
  This method is used to set the date and time as in
  timestamp format, which is the number of
  milliseconds passed since since January 1, 1970.

Example:

```
var myDate = new Date();
myDate.setTime(1500286895000 ); // 2017-07-
17T10:21:35Z
```

Please note that the above-mentioned method sets the component of the date relative to the local time zone, if you want them with respect to UTC you can just add the word "UTC" after the "get" part of the method in the above-mentioned methods, for example "setMinutes()" becomes "setUTCMinutes()".

# The Date.now() method

If you want to get current the time as the number of milliseconds passed since January 1, 1970, then you do not need to create a new date object and then use .getTime() method on it. You can do it via Date.now() method directly.

Example:

console.log( Date.now() ); // outputs current time as no. Of milliseconds passed since January 1, 1970

The Date.parse() method

This method parses the date string passed as its argument and returns it as the number of milliseconds passed since January 1, 1970, i.e., as a timestamp. The date string must

be in a valid format. The valid forms of date strings have been explained earlier in this chapter.
Example:

```
var example = Date.parse('2017-07-17T10:21:35Z' );
console.log( example ); // 1500286895000
```

If the date string is in invalid format then thsi method returns 'NaN'.

The toDateString() method

This method is used to convert the date to a string which is in more readable form.
Example:

```
var example = Date.parse( '2017-07-17T10:21:35Z' );
console.log( example.toDateString() ); // Mon Jul 17 2017
```

This method returns the string which is relative to the local time zone, if you want to use string which is relative to UTC then you can use .toUTCString() method whose usage is same as this method.

Comparing two dates

It is really easy to compare two dates in JavaScript, it can be done just as you compare two integers with the comparison operators. Example:

```
var date1 = new Date(2017, 5, 10);
var date2 = new Date(2011, 4, 9);
if(date1 > date2) // comparing dates
        console.log("date1 is bigger!");
else
        console.log("date2 is bigger");
```

This chapter showed how to work with date and time in JavaScript.

# CHAPTER 15

# EVENTS IN JAVASCRIPT

What is an Event in JavaScript?

It's very similar to the literal meaning of the word. If anything happens that changes the DOM (Document Object Model) tree's structure, it is an event. Some of these events are generated by the user itself, like Mouse events or Keyboard events while some events are generated by the browser API itself, like scrolling to a particular area of the web page or play/pause of a video, page reloads, or window resizes, etc. These events have their properties or attributes and are prototyped to contain a function/method which is fired when the property/attribute/value of a particular event changes, either by the user or automated.

These events allow developers to execute code when that event happens. This allows greater flexibility to the developers and smooth usability to the end user.

When the end user does something on the web page, an event is said to take place. In addition to user-initiated events, there are some events like "load" which is executed when the page has finished loading, for instance.

Example:

```
<p> This is a paragraph </p>
<script language = "text/javascript">
addEventListener("click", function(){
console.log("You clicked!");
</script>
```

This code snippet adds an "Event Listener" to the DOM element <p> and attaches an anonymous function which gets called when the element is clicked, and the console displays "You clicked!" when that happens. The event handler for a specific event to take place and when it happens, it handles the event by executing the code that the anonymous function has within itself:

# Earlier event handling methods

In the initial days when the event-handling was being developed, it supported just a handful of events. The mouseover and mouseout events were very successful and gained popularity instantly and were on every other page. Apart from that, there was the addition of the event handler that could detect whether the user had submitted a form and executed functions when it detected true.

These initial events led to a revolution, and an enormous set of events developed were released later. The interaction was not limited to something. Developers could now make the web page come alive and react to different user actions.

A typical event handler back in the hay days looked somewhat like this:

```
<a href="#" onclick='alert("Clicked");'>
```

# Event handling today

The number of events that a typical modern browser supports today has grown to an enormous extent if compared to the 2000s. Also, back then most of the event handlers were spilled here and there on anchor links and buttons on the HTML code, and it was very absurd to even look at, let alone debug. Today, almost every event handler can be coded entirely in the JavaScript file. We don't have to clutter up the HTML code. Further, we have also been given the freedom to attach multiple event handlers that were not possible back then.

## Event objects

The built-in function addEventListener() takes in two arguments, the first one being the Event object. Event object gives us the information about the event in the form of an object, like, say click, scrollTop, mousedown, mouseover, etc. For example, in the previous example if we were to know what button was clicked, we can look at the object's *which* property.

```
<button> Click me any way you want </button>
<script>
var button = document.querySelector("button");
button.addEventListener("mousedown",
function(event){
 if(event.which==1)
  console.log("Left Button");
else if(event.which==2)
```

```
  console.log("Middle Button");
else if(event.which==3)
  console.log("Right Button");
});
</script>
```

The information stored in an event object differs per type of event. The object's typeproperty always holds a string identifying the event.

Let's look at some common HTML5 events:

- Mouse Events
- Keyboard Events
- Browser Events
- Form Events
- CSS Animation Events
- CSS Transition Events
- Media Events
- Progress Events

# Mouse events

The mouse events are fired when the system detects a change in position/state of the pointing device over the element that has the listener attached to it.

1) mouseenter
   - This event is fired when the mouse is moved over any element with the listener is attached to. It acts in a way similar to how :hover pseudo-class in CSS works.
     Eg: <a href="#" onmouseenter=someFunc() > Element </a>
2) mouseover
   - This event is fired when the pointing device is moved onto the element that has the listener attached to itself or any one of its child elements.
3) mouseup/mousedown
   - This event is fired when the mouse is pressed on an element and the mousedown fires when the mouse is released over an element.
4) click
   - This event is fired when the mouse button (Right or Left) has been pressed and released on an element

5) dblclick
   - This event is fired when the mouse button (ANY) has been clicked twice on the element.
6) wheel
   - This event is fired when the wheel button of the mouse is rotated in any direction.
7) mouseleave
   - This event is fired when the mouse leaves the element to which the listener was attached to.

## Keyboard Events

These are the events when the system detects the change in the state of the keys of a keyboard

1) keydown
   - When any key is pressed on the keyboard, this event is fired.
2) keypress
   - When any key except some special keys like Shift, Fn, CapsLock is in pressed manner, this event takes place.
3) keyup
   - When any key is released from a pressed state, this event takes place.

# Browser events

Some events do not adhere to what the user clicks or makes changes to, but rather the

change in the state of some resources native to the browser

1) cached
    - This event is fired when the resources that were necessary for the page load completes downloading, and the application caching is done.
2) error
    - This event is fired if a resource failed to load.
3) abort
    - This event is fired when the loading of any particular resource has been aborted.
4) load
    - This event is fired when the document finishes loading.
5) beforeunload
    - This event is fired when the document and all of its resources are about to be unloaded.
6) unload

- This event is fired when the document is being unloaded from the disk cache.

## Form Events

Forms are central to making dynamic pages.

1) reset
   - This event is fired when the reset button is pressed, i.e. the form is reset.
2) submit
   - This event is fired when the form is being submitted so that some required action can be taken via event handlers.
3) onblur
   - This event is fired when the element loses focus
4) onchange
   - This event is fired when the content of the form event is altered.
5) onfocus
   - This event is fired when the element gets focus
6) oninput

- This event is fired when the element gets some input from the user.

## CSS animation events

The animations done with the help of CSS makes the page pretty, and when we are

able to know the states of the animation, we can govern it using these events

1) animationstart
   - This event is fired when a CSS animation has started. If there is some animation-delay, this event will fire once the delay time is done with.
2) animationend
   - This event is fired once the animation stops.

3) animationiteration
   - When the CSS animation is repeated, this event is fired.

## CSS Transition events

A smooth transition made possible using CSS can be further controlled using JavaScript event handlers.

1) transitionstart
    - This event is fired when the CSS transition has actually started.

2) transitioncancel
    - This event is fired when the CSS transition has been canceled.

3) transitionend
    - This event is fired when the CSS transition has completed its course of run.

4) transitionrun
    - This event is fired when the CSS transition has starting to run before any delay whatsoever.

## Media events

There are various events that fall in this category. The most important and most used among them being:

1) play
    - This event is fired when the playback of any media begins

2) pause

- This event is fired when the media playback is paused.

3) loadmetadata
- This event is fired when the metadata has finished loading.

This is a brief list of events that are commonly used in JavaScript. There are, in addition to these, a huge list of events that the modern browser is capable of handling.

To sum it up, events in JavaScript are composed of two things:

1) Event listeners
2) Event handler

## Listening for events

As has been previously stated, everything that one does inside the web browser results in some events getting fired so that we get some response and the interactivity between the user and the application stays alive. Sometimes, events fire when the page loads. Sometimes, they fire for some particular action that you, like click a button or hover over some element or submit a form, etc.

But, what we look for is to make some of the events that hold some value to us, be commanded over, i.e. execute some task if that specific event occurs. So, we gracefully attach an event listener to that event.

The basic syntax of an event listener is like this:

source.addEventListener(eventName,       eventHandler, false);

Let's break it down and analyze it part-by-part.

1) Source
    - Source is typically any DOM element that we would want to listen for events on. For instance, an anchor link or even window object, etc.

2) The eventName
    - The function addEventListener is a built-in function that takes three arguments, the first one of which the event name which is the name of the event that we're looking to listen to, like click, mouseover, etc.

3) The eventHandler

-This is the second argument that the addEventListener function takes which is the function or chunk of code that is to be executed when the event that we're interested in fires. These are almost always anonymous functions.

Simple Example:
document.addEventListener("click", changeColor, false);

The source here, in which we're interested in is the document itself. We're attaching the event with the name click, and the event handler that handles the event is changeColor which can be defined by the user.

So far, we have listened for an event using the addEventListener function. Now, it's time to react to that event. That means that we need to define what happens when that event is fired. In this particular example, we've set the event-handler to be a function changeColor. Let's now define it.

```
function changeColor(){
        console.log("changed the color");
```

}

# Event arguments

The event handler function after getting called by an event listener also provides access to the event object as one of its arguments. This event object has properties which are exclusive to that specific event.

A mouse event object will have different properties than a keyboard event object or a browser event object. These objects have their own specialized behavior that we can exploit.

To access this event object, we need to pass it to the event handler as an argument. Preferably the letter "e" is used to indicate the event as an argument.

```
function changeColor(e){
        console.log("changed the color");
}
```

All these events have some properties/attributes in common. The major reason is that all these events are derived from the basic Event type which has been discussed earlier. Some of these events are:

1) preventDefault
2) target
3) type
4) target
5) stopPropagation
6) currentTarget

## Removing an event listener

When there's a need to add some event listeners to some DOM element, there is an equal need to remove these listeners from the elements. This is done using the removeEventListener() function whose basic structure and signature is basically the same as addEventListener().

source.removeEventListener(eventName, eventHandler, false);

# CONCLUSION

That should give you a basic idea of how events are used in JavaScript and why is it necessary to use them in the first place. The things to note are that events are anything that happens in the application, and we can attach event-listeners to make sure we get to know when that event occurs so that we can execute some code at that time.

Thank you very much for downloading JavaScript: Beginner JavaScript Coding From The Ground Up! Please be on the lookout for the next book in this series, JavaScript: Intermediate JavaScript Coding From The Ground Up. There is more yet left to learn to further your coding knowledge base. The journey does not stop at beginner for us.

If you have enjoyed this book, please leave a positive review on Amazon to show your support. Your feedback is greatly appreciated!